What's in this book

This book belongs to

_____

新同学 New schoolmates

学习内容 Contents

沟通 Communication

说说位置
Talk about locations

生词 New words

★	新	new
★	旧	old
★	左边	left
★	右边	right
★	桌子	desk
★	但是	but
★	妹妹	younger sister
	班	class
	年级	grade
	教室	classroom
	椅子	chair
	找	to look for

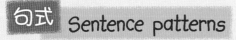 **Sentence patterns**

大卫想去找妹妹，但是他不知道她在哪里。

David wants to find his younger sister but he doesn't know where she is.

文化 **Cultures**

中国的初等教育
Primary education in China

跨学科学习 **Project**

比较电脑教室
Compare computer classrooms

Get ready

1. Do you have any new schoolmates?

2. What do you do when you meet new schoolmates?

3. Do you think Hao Hao and his friends like the new schoolmates?

bān
班

xīn
新

班上来了一个新同学，他叫大卫。
大家都很喜欢他。

大卫坐在浩浩的前面，他的左边是
爱莎，右边是艾文。

下课了，大卫想去找妹妹，但是他不知道她在哪里。

nián jí
年级

Grade 1 一年级

"我们带你去。"大家说。
"谢谢！她读一年级。"大卫说。

教室

"哥哥，我在这里！"大卫妹妹说。
"你的教室真可爱。"大卫说。

jiù
旧

zhuō zi
桌子

yǐ zi
椅子

"这是我们的旧教室，桌子、椅子还是和以前一样。"大家说。

Let's think

1 Recall the story. Put a tick or a cross.

2 There are many different classroom seating plans. Can you draw yours?

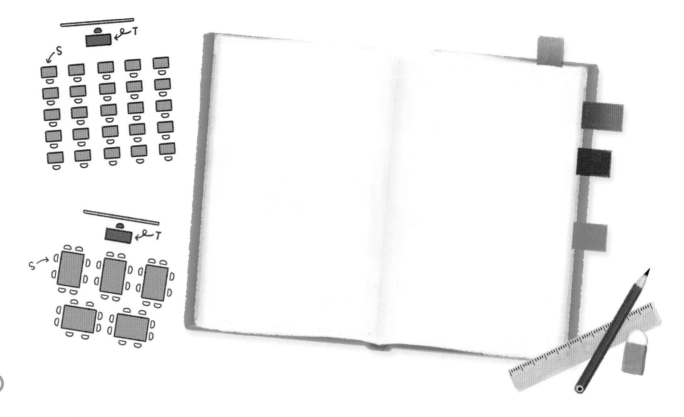

New words

02 1 Learn the new words.

新　左边　年级　班　旧　右边　一年级A班　但是　妹妹　找　椅子　桌子　教室

2 Say the words to your friend and ask him/her to point to the correct words in the picture above.

🎧03 1 Listen and write the letters.

🎧04 2 Look at the pictures. Listen to the story an

1 我喜欢我的 ___，
  它是爸爸给我的。

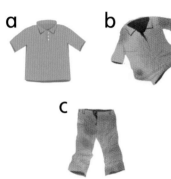

a   b

c

2 他是我的同学，坐
  在我的 ___ 边。

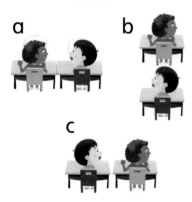

a   b

c

3 她是大卫的 ___，
  她比大卫小三岁。

a   b

c

①

🗨 大卫，你怎么了？

🗨 我想去洗手间，但是不知道在哪里。

③ 洗手间   一年级A班

🗨 在我妹妹教室的左边吗？

🗨 是的。

y.

洗手间在一年级A班教室的
左边。

那很好找。谢谢你，爱莎。

不客气！

3 Write the letters and say.

a 左边　b 右边　c 但是
d 新　　e 妹妹　f 桌子

我有哥哥和
姐姐，___我
没有妹妹。

这是我和___的卧室。
我们的床在___，___
和椅子在___。

这是我的___
雨伞，我很喜
欢它的颜色。

Task

Paste or draw a picture of your classroom and talk about the classrooms with your friend.

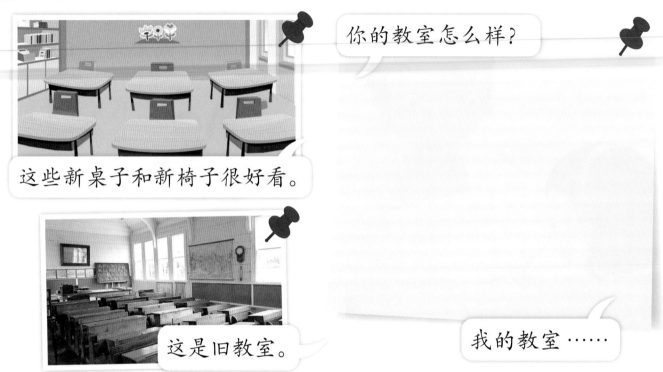

你的教室怎么样？

这些新桌子和新椅子很好看。

这是旧教室。

我的教室……

Game

Say the words and act it out. Can you get them all right?

上

下

前

后

左

右

Chant

05 Listen and say.

我们的学校有很多教室，

新桌子、新椅子大家都喜欢。

我们的学校有很多年级，

哥哥、姐姐、弟弟、妹妹一起来学习。

你坐我左边，我坐你右边，

我们一起好好学习，天天真开心！

生活用语 Daily expressions

你找谁？
Who are you looking for?

我带你去。
I will take you there.

15

写一写 Write

1 Trace and write the characters.

一 ナ 左 左 左

一 ナ 右 右 右

左 右 左 右

丨 ⺊ 占 占 占 卓 卓 桌

桌 桌 桌 桌

2 Write and say.

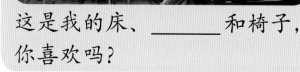

男孩在小狗＿＿边。
小狗在男孩＿＿边。

这是我的床、＿＿＿＿＿和椅子，
你喜欢吗？

3 Fill in the blanks with the correct words. Colour the school bags using the same colours.

人   比   他们   好看   桌子

_____是英国___。这是他
们的教室。教室里的_____和椅
子是蓝色的。他们的教室___我
们的教室_____吗?

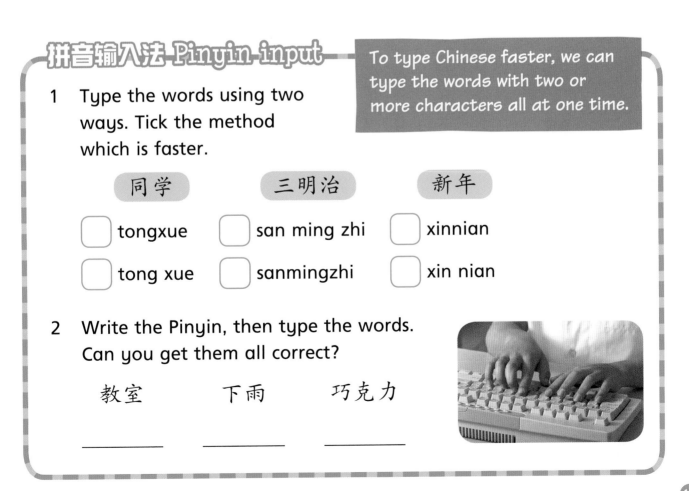

To type Chinese faster, we can type the words with two or more characters all at one time.

1 Type the words using two ways. Tick the method which is faster.

同学   三明治   新年

☐ tongxue   ☐ san ming zhi   ☐ xinnian

☐ tong xue   ☐ sanmingzhi   ☐ xin nian

2 Write the Pinyin, then type the words. Can you get them all correct?

教室   下雨   巧克力

_____   _____   _____

Cultures

1 What do primary students in China do at school? Is their school system different from yours?

In China, primary education is a part of the Nine-year Compulsory Education. It usually lasts for six years with two terms in each school year. All children must attend primary school at age 6 or 7.

2 Compare the subjects in schools in China with your school. Circle the ones which are different.

Primary school subjects in China

音乐 Music

数学 Mathematics

科学 Science

外语 Foreign Language

语文 Chinese

体育 PE (Physical Education)

美术 Arts

品德与社会 Moral Education and Social Studies

1 Paste a photo of your computer classroom below. Look at the photos and talk about the classrooms with your friend.

Paste your photo here.

我喜欢左边的电脑教室。

右边是我的电脑教室。

我喜欢这些桌子、椅子、电脑。

这些电脑……

四个同学坐在一起。

我喜欢在……

2 What lessons are the children having? Type the subjects in Chinese. Say to your friend.

美术

音乐

数学

温习 Checkpoint

1 Follow the arrows and complete the tasks in the classrooms. Then go to the main door and take the school bus home.

大卫想找妹妹，但是他不知道她在哪里。

爱莎在大卫的 □ 边，艾文在大卫的 □ 边。

Which grade are you in? Answer in Chinese.

What is the name of your class? Answer in Chinese.

她是大卫的什么人？

他叫什么名字？

这是 □ 子。

20

2 Work with your friend. Colour the stars and the chillies.

Words and sentences	说	读	写
新	☆	☆	🌶
旧	☆	☆	🌶
左边	☆	☆	☆
右边	☆	☆	☆
桌子	☆	☆	☆
但是	☆	☆	🌶
妹妹	☆	☆	🌶
班	☆	🌶	🌶
年级	☆	🌶	🌶
教室	☆	🌶	🌶
椅子	☆	🌶	🌶
找	☆	🌶	🌶
大卫想去找妹妹，但是他不知道她在哪里。	☆	☆	🌶

Talk about locations	☆

3 What does your teacher say?

分享 Sharing

Words I remember

新	xīn	new
旧	jiù	old
左边	zuǒ biān	left
右边	yòu biān	right
桌子	zhuō zi	table
但是	dàn shì	but
妹妹	mèi mei	younger sister
班	bān	class
年级	nián jí	grade
教室	jiào shì	classroom
椅子	yǐ zi	chair
找	zhǎo	to find

Other words

坐	zuò	to sit
想	xiǎng	to want to
带	dài	to take
读	dú	to read
以前	yǐ qián	before
品德	pǐn dé	Moral Education
社会	shè huì	Social Studies
科学	kē xué	Science
音乐	yīn yuè	Music
体育	tǐ yù	PE (Physical Education)
语文	yǔ wén	Chinese Language
外语	wài yǔ	Foreign Language

OXFORD
UNIVERSITY PRESS

Oxford University Press is a department of the University of Oxford.
It furthers the University's objective of excellence in research, scholarship,
and education by publishing worldwide. Oxford is a registered trade mark of
Oxford University Press in the UK and in certain other countries

Published in Hong Kong by
Oxford University Press (China) Limited
39th Floor, One Kowloon, 1 Wang Yuen Street, Kowloon Bay,
Hong Kong

Illustrated by Anne Lee, Emily Chan, KY Chan and Wildman

Photographs for reproduction permitted by Dreamstime.com

China National Publications Import & Export (Group) Corporation is an authorized distributor of
Oxford Elementary Chinese.

Please contact content@cnpiec.com.cn or 86-10-65856782

ISBN: 978-0-19-082254-5

10 9 8 7 6 5 4 3 2